CREATIVE VIBES ONLY®

CreativeVibesOnly.com

@CreativeVibes.Only

@Creative_ian

Be Here, Be now.
Mindful Moments of Coloring for your wellness, creativity and presence.

CREATIVE VIBES ONLY®

For more information, address: info@CreativeVibesOnly.com.

PO Box 1649
New York, NY 10027

First paperback edition November 2022

Cover designed by Booklerk
Mandalas designed by Maria Holm
Designs by Pan Agustus

ISBN 979-8-985-16963-8 (paperback)

Published by CREATIVE VIBES ONLY, LLC.
An imprint of Age of The Creative™

CreativeVibesOnly.com

BE HERE, BE NOW.

CREATIVES! I know how demanding, rewarding, stressful, joyous, annoying yet fulfilling your days and life may be working to create change, new things and do the things you love. I created this coloring book in and with love for you noting all of the above..

May this journal help your daily vibe, support your creativity and make you a better human.

May you be safe,

May you be happy in and with your creativity,

May you be healthy,

May your capabilities be free from pain, suffering or sorrow.

May your gifts make room for you,

May you create and use your creativity with ease.

May you be mindful, present, go within and continue to help yourself.

– Ian D.

Foreword to Be Here, Be Now

A mandala is an art form intended to focus our attention. You can think of it as a visual mindfulness aid. The circular shape of the mandala is like a map, a map that can lead us back to ourselves. For centuries, mandalas have acted as portals to our inner emotional world.

What you hold in your hands is a time portal. Within the pages that follow you will find portals to a world of your own making. Right now, there are many things vying for your time and attention. By choosing to spend a few minutes of your day coloring, you have given yourself a very precious gift: The gift of intentionally focused time. When we take time out of our day to color, we are allowing ourselves to be fully present to the joy of coloring.

In my work as a licensed Creative Arts Therapist (LCAT), I help people tap into the wisest, most creative parts of themselves in order to move past life's challenges. So, when Ian Davis asked me to write the foreword to this mindful coloring journal, I was overjoyed! This is because coloring a mandala is a simple, fun way for us to regulate our nervous system. Through the process of coloring, we can engage our sense of touch, invite color into our sense of sight, and tune into the sound of our pencils or crayons.

To be sure, the texture of the media you use will give each page a particular feel. With colored pencils we can be more precise with our lines, patiently building up a block of color through repeated strokes. Noticing the rhythm of those strokes can be a mindfulness practice. With a buttery, waxy crayon we get to return to the playfulness of our youth. The texture and feel of using crayon will be much different than that of the colored pencil.

Be Here, Be Now invites you to explore and to be present with each exploration. The journal pages leave space for you to process and to reflect along the way. Take your time with each page of this coloring journal. You may be surprised at what you discover.

Paul Singleton III, LCAT ATR CMT

Before you dive in, here's some information that can help in your process and journey to presence, awareness and wellbeing as you use this coloring book.

MINDFULNESS

What is it?

Mindfulness is A present moment awareness cultivation — A way of paying attention purposefully in the moment with kindness(no judgment).

Mindfulness Meditation is and are those self-regulation practices that focus on training attention and awareness in order to bring mental processes under greater voluntary control and thereby foster general mental well-being and development and/or specific capacities such as calmness, clarity and concentration.

There are myriad of benefits of Mindfulness and Mindfulness Meditation practices, that science has proven like:

- Strengthens the brain's ability to focus on one thing and ignore distractions.
- Puts an end to limited thinking
- Helps us appreciate the well-being that is already there
- Notice whether our thinking is useful or not
- Remember to come back to the present moment

- Foster and boost general mental well-being
- Cultivate cognitive development and emotional intelligence
- Control and slow your breath rate
- Easily raise your energy and vibration
- Stress reactivity
- Better focus on your creativity
- Enhanced sleep

- Improve present moment awareness
- Reduces Stress -- reduced the inflammatory response caused by stress
- Promotes emotional health, decreasing depression.

WHAT IS A MINDFUL MOMENT?

Mindful Moments are *activities and exercises for the creative community to explore ways to improve mindfulness and restore feelings of well-being, daily.*

How Can Mindful Moments and Activities Help Me, My Creativity and My Mindfulness?
There are a myriad of Mindful and mindfulness practices like mindful walking, mindfulness meditation and mindful eating that naturally help you cultivate a state of presence, awareness and focus. Coloring has the ability to relax the fear center of your brain, the amygdala. It induces the same state as meditating by reducing the thoughts of a restless mind. This generates mindfulness and quietness which allows your mind to get some rest after a long day at work.

Coloring goes beyond being a fun activity for relaxation. It requires the two hemispheres of the brain to communicate. While logic helps us stay inside the lines, choosing colors generates a creative thought process.

GUIDE TO BE HERE, BE NOW MINDFUL COLORING:

1. Sit quietly for a few minutes and observe your feelings, the space around you and the objects you intend to color.

2. Before putting colored pencil, marker, brush, crayon or to paper, how do you feel?
How do the paper, markers or tools feel in your hands? Try to look at everything in a way you haven't before. What do you see that you have never noticed before?

3. When you are ready, start to Color. Be non-critical and remain non-judgmental about your own abilities.
It can be difficult, but the absence of judgment is an intrinsic part of mindful practice. Avoid thinking about previous experiences, telling yourself that you're not artistic, can't color well, etc. thinking too much about the end result will take you out of the moment and what's happening.

4. Think outside the box.
There are many techniques that can encourage more abstract creative thinking and mindfulness. Try an approach to coloring or painting that you haven't before – maybe using dots instead of traditional shading techniques will add a new dimension to coloring that can help improve focus.

5. There is no right or wrong way to color.
The end result isn't the primary goal with this moment; rather it is the process of being mindful and focused on the act of coloring or painting that is most important.

6. Stay present
Thinking too much will take you out of the present moment. Put yourself here and now -- do your best to avoid thinking about what happened earlier in the day or things you have to do after. It is important to stay present.

7. Noticing
As you color, notice and accept what feelings, thoughts and emotions come up for you without judgment. Keep paying attention to what arises – If it's comfortable, lean into it and let yourself flow.

8. Have compassion and gratitude on yourself
Give and show yourself some love for being here and taking the time out to invest in your wellness and Creativity.

MINDFUL MOMENTS OF COLORING FOR YOUR WELLNESS, CREATIVITY AND PRESENCE

NOTES, THOUGHTS, REFLECTIONS AND VIBES AND GRATITUDE:
What came up during this coloring session that you want to further reflect on or dive deeper into?

NOTES, THOUGHTS, REFLECTIONS AND VIBES AND GRATITUDE:
What came up during this coloring session that you want to further reflect on or dive deeper into?

NOTES, THOUGHTS, REFLECTIONS AND VIBES AND GRATITUDE
What came up during this coloring session that you want to further reflect on or dive deeper into?

NOTES, THOUGHTS, REFLECTIONS AND VIBES AND GRATITUDE:
What came up during this coloring session that you want to further reflect on or dive deeper into?

MINDFUL MOMENTS OF COLORING FOR YOUR WELLNESS, CREATIVITY AND PRESENCE

NOTES, THOUGHTS, REFLECTIONS AND VIBES AND GRATITUDE:
What came up during this coloring session that you want to further reflect on or dive deeper into?

____

____

____

____

____

____

____

____

____

____

NOTES, THOUGHTS, REFLECTIONS AND VIBES AND GRATITUDE:
What came up during this coloring session that you want to further reflect on or dive deeper into?

BE HERE, BE NOW

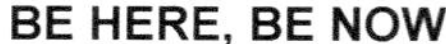

HAPPINESS
HAPPINESS
HAPPINESS
HAPPINESS
HAPPINESS
HAPPINESS

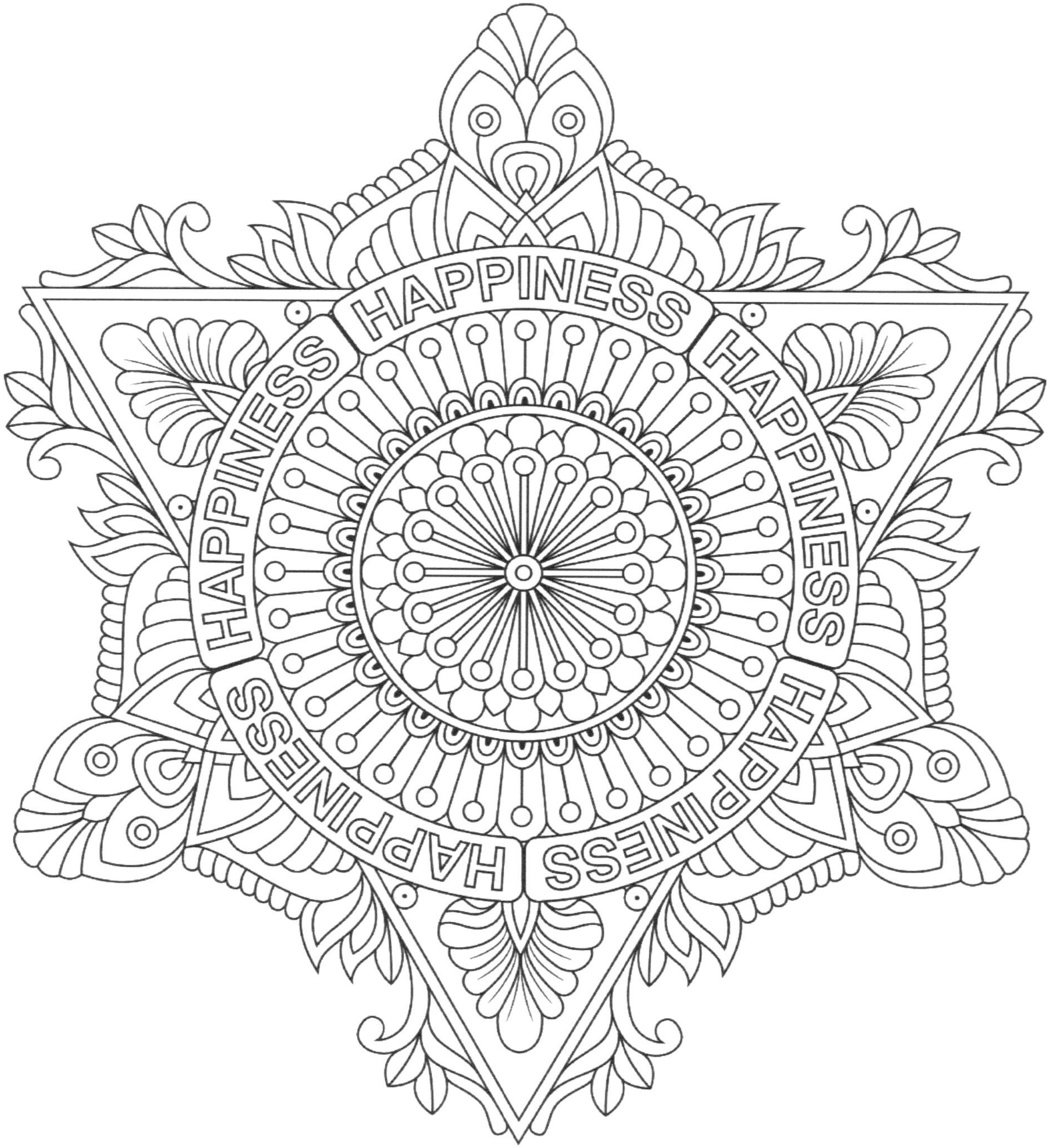

NOTES, THOUGHTS, REFLECTIONS AND VIBES AND GRATITUDE:

What came up during this coloring session that you want to further reflect on or dive deeper into?

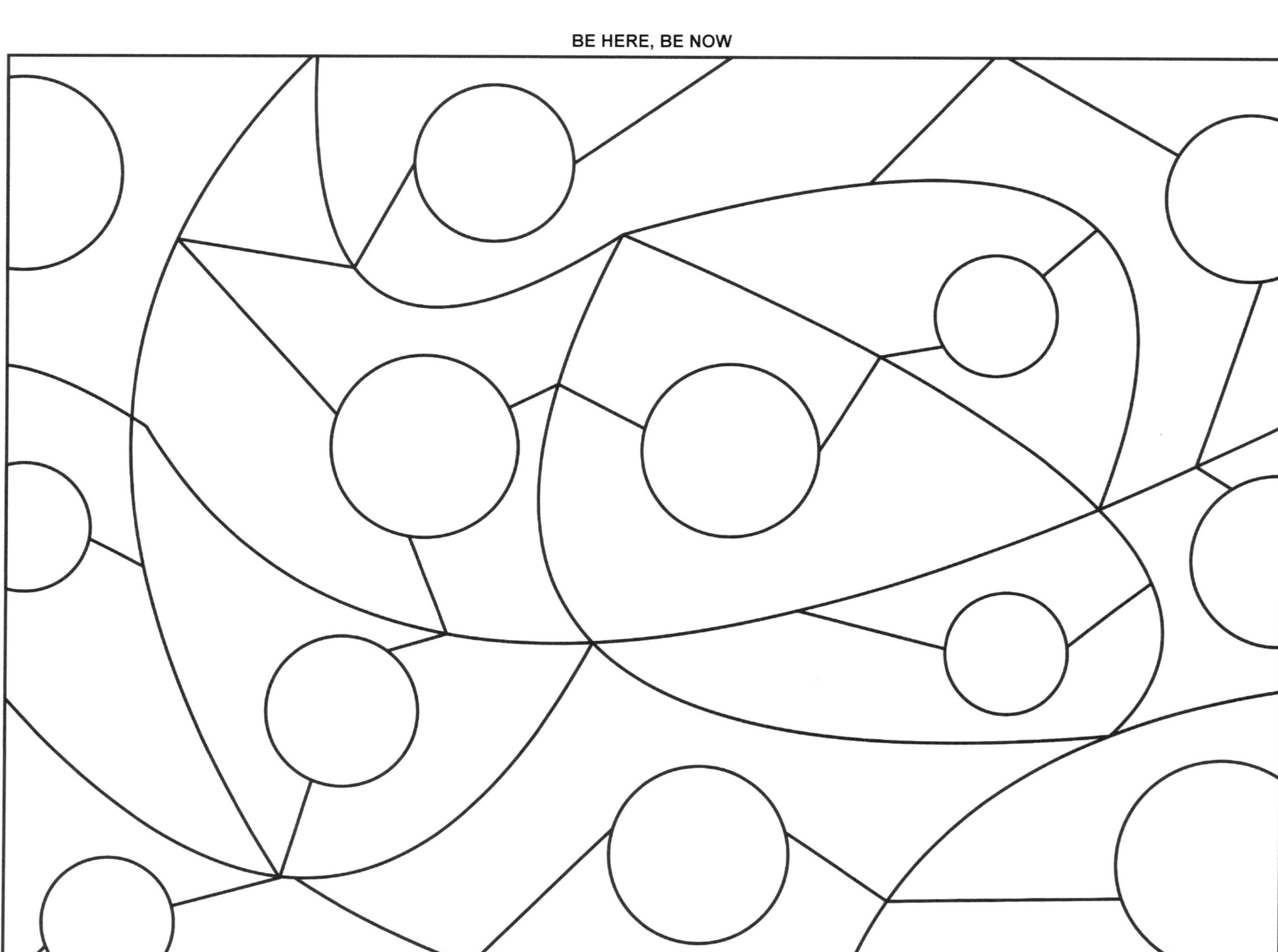

NOTES, THOUGHTS, REFLECTIONS AND VIBES AND GRATITUDE:
What came up during this coloring session that you want to further reflect on or dive deeper into?

NOTES, THOUGHTS, REFLECTIONS AND VIBES AND GRATITUDE:

What came up during this coloring session that you want to further reflect on or dive deeper into?

MINDFUL MOMENTS OF COLORING FOR YOUR WELLNESS, CREATIVITY AND PRESENCE

NOTES, THOUGHTS, REFLECTIONS AND VIBES AND GRATITUDE:
What came up during this coloring session that you want to further reflect on or dive deeper into?

MINDFUL MOMENTS OF COLORING FOR YOUR WELLNESS, CREATIVITY AND PRESENCE

NOTES, THOUGHTS, REFLECTIONS AND VIBES AND GRATITUDE:
What came up during this coloring session that you want to further reflect on or dive deeper into?

MINDFUL MOMENTS OF COLORING FOR YOUR WELLNESS, CREATIVITY AND PRESENCE

NOTES, THOUGHTS, REFLECTIONS AND VIBES AND GRATITUDE:

What came up during this coloring session that you want to further reflect on or dive deeper into?

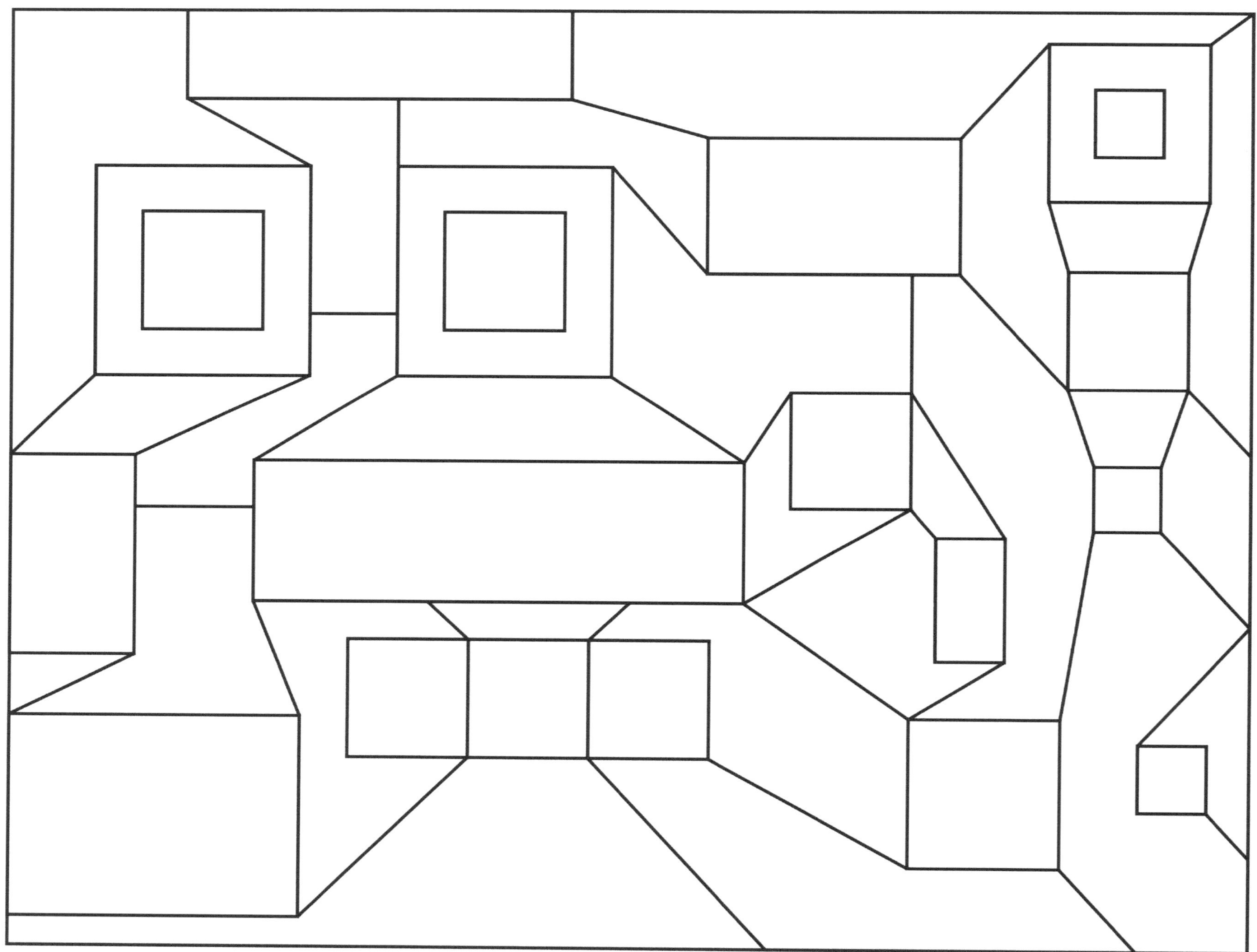

NOTES, THOUGHTS, REFLECTIONS AND VIBES AND GRATITUDE:
What came up during this coloring session that you want to further reflect on or dive deeper into?

EASE
EASE
EASE
EASE
EASE
EASE
EASE
EASE

NOTES, THOUGHTS, REFLECTIONS AND VIBES AND GRATITUDE:
What came up during this coloring session that you want to further reflect on or dive deeper into?

MINDFUL MOMENTS OF COLORING FOR YOUR WELLNESS, CREATIVITY AND PRESENCE

NOTES, THOUGHTS, REFLECTIONS AND VIBES AND GRATITUDE:
What came up during this coloring session that you want to further reflect on or dive deeper into?

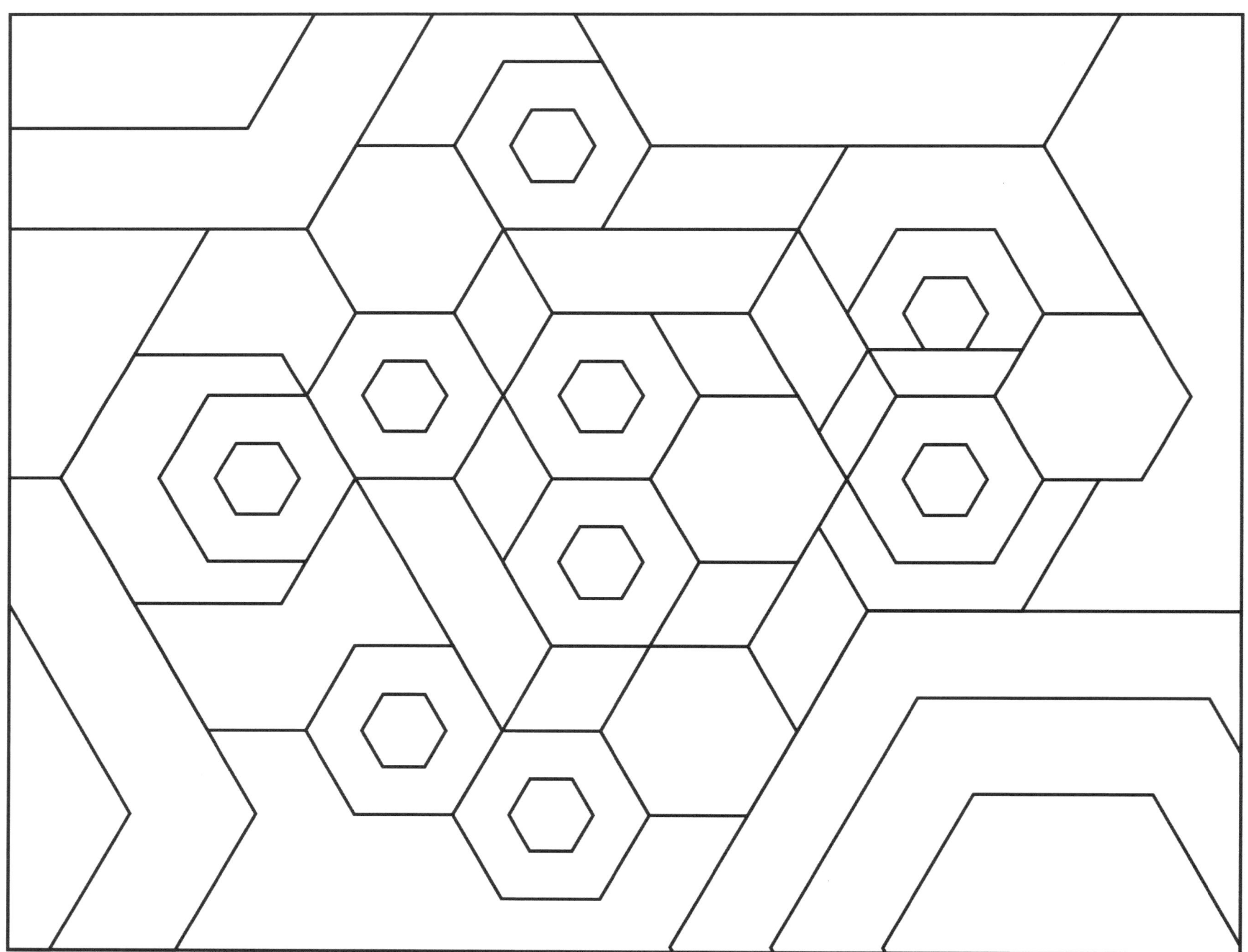

NOTES, THOUGHTS, REFLECTIONS AND VIBES AND GRATITUDE:
What came up during this coloring session that you want to further reflect on or dive deeper into?

MINDFUL MOMENTS OF COLORING FOR YOUR WELLNESS, CREATIVITY AND PRESENCE

NOTES, THOUGHTS, REFLECTIONS AND VIBES AND GRATITUDE:
What came up during this coloring session that you want to further reflect on or dive deeper into?

NOTES, THOUGHTS, REFLECTIONS AND VIBES AND GRATITUDE:
What came up during this coloring session that you want to further reflect on or dive deeper into?

MINDFUL MOMENTS OF COLORING FOR YOUR WELLNESS, CREATIVITY AND PRESENCE

NOTES, THOUGHTS, REFLECTIONS AND VIBES AND GRATITUDE:

What came up during this coloring session that you want to further reflect on or dive deeper into?

MINDFUL MOMENTS OF COLORING FOR YOUR WELLNESS, CREATIVITY AND PRESENCE

NOTES, THOUGHTS, REFLECTIONS AND VIBES AND GRATITUDE:

What came up during this coloring session that you want to further reflect on or dive deeper into?

MINDFUL MOMENTS OF COLORING FOR YOUR WELLNESS, CREATIVITY AND PRESENCE

NOTES, THOUGHTS, REFLECTIONS AND VIBES AND GRATITUDE:
What came up during this coloring session that you want to further reflect on or dive deeper into?

NOTES, THOUGHTS, REFLECTIONS AND VIBES AND GRATITUDE:
What came up during this coloring session that you want to further reflect on or dive deeper into?

MINDFUL MOMENTS OF COLORING FOR YOUR WELLNESS, CREATIVITY AND PRESENCE

NOTES, THOUGHTS, REFLECTIONS AND VIBES AND GRATITUDE:

What came up during this coloring session that you want to further reflect on or dive deeper into?

NOTES, THOUGHTS, REFLECTIONS AND VIBES AND GRATITUDE:
What came up during this coloring session that you want to further reflect on or dive deeper into?

____

____

____

____

____

____

____

____

____

____

____

MINDFUL MOMENTS OF COLORING FOR YOUR WELLNESS, CREATIVITY AND PRESENCE

NOTES, THOUGHTS, REFLECTIONS AND VIBES AND GRATITUDE:
What came up during this coloring session that you want to further reflect on or dive deeper into?

MINDFUL MOMENTS OF COLORING FOR YOUR WELLNESS, CREATIVITY AND PRESENCE

NOTES, THOUGHTS, REFLECTIONS AND VIBES AND GRATITUDE:
What came up during this coloring session that you want to further reflect on or dive deeper into?

MINDFUL MOMENTS OF COLORING FOR YOUR WELLNESS, CREATIVITY AND PRESENCE

NOTES, THOUGHTS, REFLECTIONS AND VIBES AND GRATITUDE:

What came up during this coloring session that you want to further reflect on or dive deeper into?

____

____

____

____

____

____

____

____

____

____

NOTES, THOUGHTS, REFLECTIONS AND VIBES AND GRATITUDE:

What came up during this coloring session that you want to further reflect on or dive deeper into?

____

____

____

____

____

____

____

____

____

____

____

MINDFUL MOMENTS OF COLORING FOR YOUR WELLNESS, CREATIVITY AND PRESENCE

NOTES, THOUGHTS, REFLECTIONS AND VIBES AND GRATITUDE:

What came up during this coloring session that you want to further reflect on or dive deeper into?

NOTES, THOUGHTS, REFLECTIONS AND VIBES AND GRATITUDE:

What came up during this coloring session that you want to further reflect on or dive deeper into?

Add these other books from Ian to your collection

[My] Daily Vibe: 365-day journal for creatives to be their highest and best self and the **[My] Daily Vibe Creative Companion notebooks** are an indispensable guide for anyone who wants to level up their creative game. If you like motivation, inspiration, guided journaling, and progress you can feel, get your copy of this step-by-step journal and start breaking through.

Buy **[My] Daily Vibe** to unlock the creative power within you and create your best work today at MyDailyVibe.co, Amazon, Barnes and Noble and other retailers worldwide.

www.ingramcontent.com/pod-product-compliance
Lightning Source LLC
Chambersburg PA
CBHW041034120726

48005CB00005B/808